Less
Is
More

Less Is More

101 ways to
simplify your life

Domonique
Bertolucci

Hardie Grant

B O O K S

For Sophia and Tobias

Less is more…
except when it comes to love,
and then more is more is more.

'Enjoy the little things,
for one day you may look back
and realise they were the big things.'

ROBERT BRAULT

Preface

*Trying to do it all, be it all and have it
all is exhausting. All too often people find
themselves asking, 'What was it all for?'
The sad conclusion for so many is that the
things they pushed themselves to do and have
were rarely that important and never led to
the happy and fulfilling life they longed for.*

About ten years ago, something fundamentally
shifted in the way I viewed my life. I began
my evolution from someone who loved to hit
the shops every Saturday and needed three
wardrobes to fit all her clothes to someone who
still loves beautiful things, but doesn't need
many of them to keep her satisfied.

It all started when I ended my career in banking, where massive paycheques and endless spending are a way of life, and moved back to Australia to begin my married life and start my own business.

My husband and I had only been in Sydney for a couple of days when we found our dream apartment. It was in a gorgeous Art Deco building with sweeping views of the city, Harbour Bridge and Opera House. I fell in love with it immediately and (lucky for me, given my newly married status) so did my husband. The only catch was that this apartment was tiny. Although the views gave it a sense of vastness, the rooms were minuscule and there was no storage to speak of. Undeterred, we knew we had to have it, so off to the auction we went, and a couple of nerve-racking hours later the dream home was ours.

Not long after we moved in, our 40 or so packing boxes arrived from England and it became very obvious, very quickly, that a massive clutter-clearing was in order. Once we finally had our home organised, I could see I needed to think much more carefully about what I bought: did I really need it, and where was I going to put it?

This new way of life took a bit of getting used to but my transformation was complete when I read an article about French women and their approach to their wardrobes. The French have long had a reputation for being advocates of *less is more*, whether in their stylish appearance, the restrained elegance of their homes or the small portions of indulgences on their plates.

This article began by talking about the 80–20 rule or Pareto principle*, and how most of us wear 20 per cent of our clothing 80 per cent of the time, whereas a French

---

* Named after the Italian economist Vilfredo Pareto, the Pareto principle states that for many events, roughly 80 per cent of the effects come from 20 per cent of the causes.

woman aims to only own that 20 per cent. This isn't about austerity: she may only own one scarf, but it's probably an Hermès one; one handbag but it's in the most buttery-soft leather; one pair of black trousers, but with the perfect cut and most flattering fit.

I loved the simplicity of this approach and set about streamlining my life even further, applying this philosophy not only to my wardrobe but to my whole way of living. *'Is this essential?'*, *'Is it the best it can be?'* and *'Does it really matter?'* have become questions I continually ask about everything I think or do.

I've been living this way for years now and have long given up trying to do it all, be it all or have it all.

If there is one thing I know for certain, when it comes to being happy, less is *definitely* more.

If you would like to apply this philosophy to your life, visit domoniquebertolucci.com/life and download the **Less is More Manifesto** and a range of other free resources to help you get the most out of your life.

'*Your time is limited
so don't waste it by trying to live
someone else's life.*'

STEVE JOBS

Live your life

When faced with a choice or decision in life, ask yourself, 'What will make me happiest?'

While there will always be more you can do or achieve, being happy with who you are and the life you live is the only real goal to strive for.

'Take care of your body.
It's the only place you have to live.'

JIM ROHN

Learn to stop

When you feel the urge to overindulge, be that with food, alcohol or simply overdoing the good times, stop and remind yourself that the pleasure will be short-lived but the payback will last much longer.

The key to a long and healthy life is knowing when to stop … and then doing it.

*'Start wherever you are
and start small.'*

RITA BAILEY

Narrow your focus

If you have a big goal or something substantial you want to achieve, don't let the size of your task overwhelm you.

Break it down into small, achievable chunks, then give all your attention and energy to the single task before you.

*'Simplicity is the keynote
of all true elegance.'*

Coco Chanel

Spring clean your style

If your wardrobe is overflowing but you never have anything to wear, it's time for a spring clean. Sell, donate or give away everything that doesn't fit you or flatter you. Be ruthless. If you're not sure if it suits you, it probably doesn't.

Maintain a wardrobe of a few high-quality items that make you look and feel amazing. You'll save time in the morning and you won't mind wearing the same thing regularly when you are guaranteed to look and feel good.

'You don't need endless time
and perfect conditions.
Do it now. Do it today.
Do it for twenty minutes
and watch your heart start beating.'

BARBARA SHER

Get started today

Don't let feeling unfit put you off getting
started on a health and fitness regime.
Instead of setting yourself a big goal that is
way out of reach and then giving up at the
first hurdle, make the commitment to do
something, anything, that moves your body
every single day.

If you keep active, your fitness will steadily
increase and before long those bigger goals
won't feel so far off.

'*Those who have no time*
for healthy eating
will sooner or later
have to find time for illness.'

EDWARD STANLEY

Read the label

Your body really is an amazing machine,
so be mindful of what you fuel it with.

Read the labels of all the food you
buy and don't eat anything that contains
ingredients you don't recognise or couldn't
keep in your pantry. Your body will thank
you for it.

'*Balanced relationships*
are always based in freedom,
not obligation.'

MICHAEL THOMAS SUNNARBORG

Pick up where you left off

The frequency with which you see your friends is no indicator of the quality of your friendships. So often the people you see the most can be the people whose company you care for the least.

No matter how long it has been, when you are with your true friends, time will fly; you will pick up where you left off and it will always feel like you just spoke yesterday.

*'Have nothing in your houses
that you do not know to be useful
or believe to be beautiful.'*

WILLIAM MORRIS

Pretend it's spring

Don't wait for spring to spring clean your home.

Have a regular clean-up and clear-out of things you don't need or haven't used for a while. If in doubt, ask yourself if the item in question enhances your home life or detracts from it.

You'll enjoy your living space so much more when it's free of things you no longer want or need.

*'You can still go shopping without buying,
because where buying is a matter of need,
shopping is a question of want.'*

ROBERT ROWLAND SMITH

Go window-shopping

Don't confuse the pleasure of looking at beautiful things with the desire to acquire them.

You don't need to buy something to enjoy a shopping trip. Think of it as visiting a gallery or museum. You can have a lot of fun window-shopping, enjoying all the visual delights of your favourite stores, and come back home with your money still safe in your wallet.

'*Men are not great or small
because of their material possessions.
They are great or small
because of what they are.*'

JAMES CASH PENNEY

Believe in yourself

If you find yourself thinking you need this or that in order to fit in, make the grade or be a part of things, remind yourself that nothing you can ever buy will make up for how you feel inside.

Instead of spending your money buying things to build you up, invest your energy believing in who you are.

'It's never too late
to be who you might have been.'

GEORGE ELIOT

Be the best you can be

There's no truth in the notion that you
are too old to change.

No matter how big or small the
improvement, there is no time better than
now to start making it happen.

Regardless of your age, you still have your
whole life ahead of you. Spend it enjoying
the new, improved you.

'Silence is golden.'

AMERICAN PROVERB

Embrace silence

If you live a busy life, you probably find your brain buzzing with thoughts during every waking hour.

Rather than adding to this cacophony with background music, news of the day or the latest in reality TV, turn the television or radio off and enjoy the silence.

Whilst you might not have a mute button for your own thoughts, allowing them to roam free and uninterrupted is the fastest way to get them to move on.

*'All that children need is love,
a grown-up to take responsibility for them,
and a soft place to land.'*

DEBORAH HARKNESS

Give them your love

Don't worry about buying the latest toys or gadgets for your children. Children don't need to have a lot of money spent on them. What they do need is priceless: your time, patience, comfort and love.

As long as you are giving your children these essentials, you are giving them everything they need.

*'The secret of your future
is hidden in your daily routine.'*

MIKE MURDOCK

Get a routine

So many people worry that having a routine will make them boring, when actually the opposite is true.

Not having to think about your daily essentials will leave your mind freer to explore more inspiring and imaginative thoughts. Not having to remember what you need to do and by when will leave you with more time and energy to be spontaneous. There's nothing boring about that!

'Not all those
who wander are lost.'

J.R.R. TOLKIEN

Steal a moment

When travelling to somewhere new, don't try to create an itinerary so value-filled and jam-packed that there is no time to just wander around and enjoy the scenery.

So often it's the little discoveries that you make in the spare moments on your trip that will leave the most lasting impression on your memory.

*'Don't confuse having a career
with having a life.'*

HILLARY RODHAM CLINTON

Get a life

Although your employers might try to convince you otherwise, there is more to life than work.

The only way to make sure your work doesn't take over your life is to spend less time there. Fill your life with other activities and interests so that work has no choice but to become just one small part of it.

'*As soon as you're done trying
to please everyone else
you actually have time
to make yourself happy.*'

DELANEY CURRY

Don't try to please everyone

Trying to keep everyone happy is one of the fastest ways to make yourself unhappy.

Although you might know a lot of people, there are probably only a few people who you really do love and cherish. Do what you can to bring joy and happiness to their lives and don't worry about trying to please the rest.

'Efficiency is doing the thing right.
Effectiveness is doing the right thing.'

PETER F. DRUCKER

Learn to prioritise

There will never be enough hours in the day to finish everything you would like to get done.

Before you get started on your to-do list, spend some time prioritising. A little extra time at the beginning will save you a whole lot of wasted time along the way.

'My body needs laughter
as much as it needs tears.
Both are cleansers of stress.'

MAHOGANY SILVERRAIN

Let it out

When you feel overwhelmed by stress, don't be brave and try to soldier through it. When you worry or feel stressed, tension builds in your body, and over time this can create a toxic effect if it's not released.

When you feel overwhelmed, find a way to release the tension. Your body will thank you for it.

*'That's what people who love you do.
They put their arms around you and
love you when you're not so lovable.'*

DEB CALETTI

Love unconditionally

It's easy to love someone who is behaving in a lovable way. But it's when they're not being quite so lovable that they really need it.

Love the people in your life for all that they are and with all of your heart. Loving unconditionally is the only real way to love.

'*Success is nothing more
than a few simple disciplines,
practised every day.*'

JIM ROHN

Keep it up

It's not the big things that make the difference as to whether or not you succeed in life.

It's the little things that you do – and keep doing – that determine whether you will achieve your goals or spend your life dreaming about them.

'People of balance
age as gracefully
as wines of balance.'

JOHN JORDAN

Practise moderation

Nothing is more debilitating than living a life of extremes.

If you want to live a long and healthy life, make sure you try a little bit of everything and not too much of anything.

'Life is really simple,
but we insist on making it complicated.'

Confucius

Make it easy

Don't keep struggling if something seems difficult. It really doesn't have to be.

There's a big difference between taking the easy way out and looking for a simple solution, so stop what you are doing, take a deep breath and ask yourself, 'How can I make this easier?' Then do it that way instead.

'*Some people think luxury*
is the opposite of poverty.
It is not. It is the opposite of vulgarity.'

COCO CHANEL

Make an investment

Always spend as much as you can on the best quality you can afford. You will have far fewer things, but those things will be guaranteed to look and feel good for the longest possible time.

'The groundwork
of all happiness
is health.'

JAMES LEIGH HUNT

Take care of yourself

It's hard to feel happy in your mind when you are feeling unhealthy in your body.

Instead of making your own wellbeing your lowest priority, move something else off your list so that you have time and energy to take care of something that really matters.

'All you need is love.
But a little chocolate now and then
doesn't hurt.'

CHARLES M. SCHULZ

Enjoy a little bite

Whilst you might never be able to eat too much broccoli or cucumber, most people can't say the same for their favourite indulgence, whether it's wine, cheese or chocolate (to name just a few).

Rather than overdoing it on cheap and cheerful varieties, treat yourself to a small portion of something exceptional. Regardless of your vice, choose the best and savour the experience.

*'Life runs in a narrow path
to balancing act, convincing tact,
and satisfying fact.'*

SANTOSH KALWAR

Tread gently

When it comes to friendship, honesty isn't always the best policy. Sometimes the last thing a friend needs to hear is the facts as you see them.

If you think a friend needs to hear some cold hard truths, warm them up first with tact and diplomacy. Then deliver them in a kind and compassionate way.

*'The time to repair the roof
is when the sun is shining.'*

JOHN F. KENNEDY

Fix it quick

Repair or replace things that are broken as soon as possible.

It's always annoying to discover something is broken when you go to use it, or – even worse – to spend weeks or even months complaining about something that could have been fixed quickly and simply at the time.

*'Hanging onto a bad buy
will not redeem the purchase.'*

TERENCE CONRAN

Get rid of it

If you buy something and it turns out not to be suitable, return it. If you can't return it, sell it, and if you can't sell it, give it away!

The only thing worse than wasting your money on an erroneous purchase is having it lying around, continually reminding you of your mistake.

'The secret of happiness, you see,
is not found in seeking more,
but in developing the capacity to enjoy less.'

SOCRATES

You have what you need

Ask yourself, 'What do I need to be happy?' Chances are not only do you need very little, but you actually already have most of it.

While you might have a long list of wants, recognise these for what they are. Don't let them get in the way of your happiness.

'*You can have it all,*
you just can't have it all at once.'

OPRAH WINFREY

Manage your expectations

If you find yourself feeling annoyed or frustrated with yourself because you haven't achieved all that you had hoped to in life by now, stop. Chances are your expectations were never realistic in the first place.

It's true that with hard work and commitment you can get many things you want from life. But no matter how hard you work or how committed you are, you still can't achieve the impossible.

'*A little while alone in your room*
will prove more valuable
than anything else that
could ever be given you.'

RUMI

Recharge your batteries

When you live a busy life, it's important to take time out to unwind. Regularly.

Rather than waiting until your stress levels are at their peak, make time each day to sit quietly and relax, regardless of whether or not you feel like you need to.

'*The soul is healed*
by being with children.'

FYODOR DOSTOYEVSKY

Earn their love

Don't expect your children to be perfect.
They've no more chance of that than you
have. Instead, love your children for who
they are, faults and all, and hope that they
do the same for you.

There is nothing quite so wonderful as the
unconditional love of a child, and the best
way to encourage that is to give it in return.

*'What is not started today
is never finished tomorrow.'*

JOHANN WOLFGANG VON GOETHE

Get it done

Having a big list of things to do is rarely inspiring, but staring at your to-do list, knowing that you are never going to get through it all and hoping that things will miraculously disappear from it, won't change anything.

Determine what you really need to get done today and create a fresh, much shorter list that you can confidently work your way through.

'*The real voyage of discovery
consists not in seeking new landscapes,
but in having new eyes.*'

MARCEL PROUST

Open your eyes

When you are on holiday, don't fall into the trap of complaining about the things that are different from home.

Make the assumption that things *will* be different when you are away, and rather than bemoan the things that you miss, open your eyes to the new things you can discover.

*'If you commit to giving more time
than you have to spend,
you will constantly be running
from time debt collectors.'*

ELIZABETH GRACE SAUNDERS

Keep some time up your sleeve

There is no such thing as a five-minute task. The thing you think will take five minutes will always take at least fifteen. And it's no different for longer tasks.

Always allow more time than you need and plan to do less than you think is possible. That way you will always have extra time up your sleeve when you inevitably discover that you need it.

'You cannot be all things to all people.
Be unique. Be different.
Give to others what you want yourself.
And do what you were made to do.'

ROBERT KIYOSAKI

Just say no

Don't try to be all things to all people. It's okay to say 'no' sometimes. In fact, it's okay to say 'no' whenever you want to.

When someone asks you to do something, swallow your instant reply and ask yourself, 'Is this something I want to do, something I need to do or something I have to do?' If you can't answer 'yes' to any of these questions, your answer is definitely 'no'.

'Organise, don't agonise.'

NANCY PELOSI

Schedule it in

If there are important things you need to do regularly – bills to pay, medical check-ups, birthday gifts to buy or trips to the dentist – avoid keeping them all in your head and fretting you might forget; instead, schedule them in your diary.

This small bit of forward planning will save you time, money, energy and embarrassing mistakes.

'If the problem can be solved, why worry?
If the problem cannot be solved,
worrying will do you no good.'

ŚĀNTIDEVA

Don't worry

Worrying about something will never change anything.

If you are feeling stressed or concerned, there are really only two options available to you. If there is something you can do, take action. If there is nothing you can do, accept it. Whatever you do, don't worry.

'Real love amounts to
withholding the truth,
even when you're offered
the perfect opportunity
to hurt someone's feelings.'

DAVID SEDARIS

Give them your best

Give the people you love the best of you, not the worst.

So often people treat their loved ones with less kindness or consideration than they do people who are barely more than acquaintances.

Give the people you love your patience and respect, and the generosity of your spirit. And keep any unkind thoughts you have to yourself.

*'Happiness is that state
of consciousness which proceeds
from the achievement of one's values.'*

AYN RAND

Focus on what matters

You don't need a lot to be happy. You just need to have the things that matter to you.

Take the time to identify and understand your values. Then honour them by integrating them into every part of your life.

'The road to health for everyone
is through moderation, harmony,
and a "sound mind in a sound body".'

JOSTEIN GAARDER

Rest your mind

While most people realise they need to take care of their body, taking care of your mental health is something that is often taken for granted.

Be vigilant about your mental and emotional wellbeing, and make sure to nurture your heart and rest your mind when they need it.

*'Do not wait until the conditions
are perfect to begin.
Beginning makes the conditions perfect.'*

ALAN COHEN

Begin it now

If there is something you want to achieve in life, there is no better place to begin than where you are right now.

All too often people put off beginning while they wait for some magical sense that 'the time is right'. But the only real right time to begin is *right now*.

'*One is never overdressed*
or underdressed
with a Little Black Dress.'

KARL LAGERFELD

Keep it simple

Feeling well dressed can give your confidence a huge boost, especially if you are feeling uncomfortable or uncertain.

If you have an event coming up that's making you feel nervous, don't overcompensate by overdressing. Keep it simple … you'll never look inappropriate in something elegant and timeless.

'Motivation is what gets you started.
Habit is what keeps you going.'

JIM RYAN

Create good habits

You don't need a lot of motivation to exercise regularly. All you need is enough motivation to keep you going until your new habit kicks in.

After all, it's no harder to create good habits than it is bad.

'*When walking, walk.*
When eating, eat.'

ZEN PROVERB

Enjoy your meal

Instead of working through your mealtimes in an attempt to squeeze more out of your day, stop and take the time to have a proper break.

You will find you eat less, enjoy your food more and feel satisfied sooner if you give your meal your full attention.

*'Sometimes nothing
is the best thing to say and
often the best thing to do.'*

MICHAEL THOMAS SUNNARBORG

Just listen

When someone comes to you with a problem, it's all too easy to fall into solution mode.

As good as telling someone what to do can make *you* feel, what they usually want is just to have you listen and, through your listening, have the chance to hear themselves think.

'If you are not content
with what you have,
you would not be satisfied
if it were doubled.'

CHARLES SPURGEON

Be content

Don't complain about the size of your home. Regardless of how big their house is, the truth is that most people do the majority of their living in one single room.

So while a bigger house might give you more bedrooms, storage and other surplus requirements, it's unlikely to give you any more space you'll actually live in.

'A bargain ain't a bargain
unless it's something you need.'

SIDNEY CARROLL

Leave it on the shelf

Don't fall into the trap of buying something just because it is on sale.

While stores can reduce their prices dramatically to tempt you to part with your money, unless you would have been willing to pay the full price in the first place, it's not a bargain – no matter how much they knock off.

*'One can furnish a room very luxuriously
by taking out furniture
rather than putting it in.'*

FRANCIS JOURDAIN

Leave some room

You don't need to fill your home with things to make it welcoming. Some simple flowers, a photograph or a comfortable chair are all you really need.

Rather than filling all the space in your rooms with things, leave room in the space for living.

'Life is about balance.
The good and the bad.
The highs and the lows.
The pina and the colada.'

ELLEN DEGENERES

Dust yourself off

Don't expect every day to be perfect. In a full and interesting life, there will always be ups and downs.

The quality of your life isn't determined by whether or not things ever go wrong, but rather how quickly you can dust yourself off when they do.

'In order to understand the world,
one has to turn away from it on occasion.'

ALBERT CAMUS

Have a power-down

Cast your mind back to a time before voicemail. Back then, if a person couldn't get hold of you when they wanted to, they simply tried again later. It doesn't have to be so different now.

Simply turn your phone off.

'What can you do to promote world peace?
Go home and love your family.'

MOTHER TERESA

Love is all you need

To be a happy family, you don't need to live in a big house, take grand holidays or give expensive gifts.

All a family needs in order to flourish is an abundance of love. Everything else is surplus.

'Time is what we want most,
but what we use worst.'

WILLIAM PENN

Don't waste time

One of the most common complaints people make is that they've got 'no time'. The truth is, you have plenty of time – 24 hours of it every single day – but you'll never feel like you have enough if you waste it instead of using it wisely.

Don't try to fit everything in. If you focus on doing what needs to be done, you'll never run out of time.

'*Travel makes one modest.*
You see what a tiny place
you occupy in the world.'

GUSTAVE FLAUBERT

Keep it in perspective

If you are on holiday and your travel plans are delayed, before you get angry or annoyed, stop and take a minute to realise just how fortunate you are.

In the grand scheme of things, being delayed going to or from somewhere nice is a rather pleasant problem to have.

Once you've got the issue back into perspective, you can relax and enjoy the ride … whenever it comes along.

*'Luck is where the crossroads
of opportunity and preparation meet.'*

SENECA

Be lucky

You don't need a lot of luck to get ahead in life, but you do need to make an effort to make the most of the luck you have.

Put in the groundwork, do the preparation and when a little bit of luck comes along, get ready to seize it for all it's worth.

'It is better to be alone
than in bad company.'

GEORGE WASHINGTON

Seek true friends

If you find yourself complaining incessantly about a friend after you see them or speak to them, it's probably time to review the friendship.

A true friend should enhance your life. If that's not what is happening, stay home and enjoy the company of a good book.

*'Amateurs sit and wait for inspiration,
the rest of us just get up and go to work.'*

STEPHEN KING

Get started

Whilst thinking and planning are an important part of any process, there is no time like the present to start doing whatever it is you want to do.

Make a start and see what happens. There is nothing like action to clarify the mind.

'Don't let your mind
bully your body into believing
it must carry the burden
of its worries.'

ASTRID ALAUDA

Learn to breathe

Not only is worry exhausting for your mind, it also has a debilitating effect on the body. When you find your mind turning and churning, stop for a moment and feel the effects these cyclical thoughts have on your body.

Instead of letting your mind run in exhaustive circles, start to breathe slowly and evenly. Let the calm return to your mind and the strength return to your body.

'We spend precious hours fearing the inevitable.
It would be wise to use that time
adoring our families, cherishing our friends
and living our lives.'

MAYA ANGELOU

Use each day wisely

None of us knows how long we will have in this life, so live each day as if it were your last. Call your friends, cherish your family and tell the people you love that you do.

Make sure that you live each day of your life fully, and appreciate today as a good day to be alive.

'It is good to have an end
to journey toward;
but it is the journey that matters,
in the end.'

ERNEST HEMINGWAY

Enjoy the ride

If, despite your efforts, you have failed to achieve a goal you have set, don't be too hard on yourself.

Remind yourself that what will matter at the end of your life isn't how many things you have achieved, but how much you enjoyed the things you did.

'The first wealth is health.'

Ralph Waldo Emerson

Invest in your health

Don't allow being busy at work to become an excuse for a poor diet and lack of exercise.

Although working hard might allow you to earn more, all the money in the world won't be worth a cent if you don't have your health to enjoy it.

*'We can complain
because rose bushes have thorns,
or rejoice because thorn bushes have roses.'*

ABRAHAM LINCOLN

See the upside

There will always be two ways to see everything you experience in life: the upside and the downside.

Rather than focusing on what is wrong, disappointing or frustrating about a given situation, make a point of discovering what is right.

'Over the years I have learned
that what is important in a dress
is the woman who is wearing it.'

YVES SAINT LAURENT

Wear a smile

You don't need a wardrobe full of clothes to look good. With bright eyes and a welcoming smile you will always look beautiful, regardless of what you are wearing.

*'All truly great thoughts
are conceived while walking.'*

FRIEDRICH NIETZSCHE

Get some fresh air

When you are feeling overwhelmed or confused about something, the best thing to do is stop thinking about it altogether.

Go for a walk in the fresh air and allow nature to clear your mind. You'll find the answer will often be waiting for you on your return.

'*Buy less, choose well
and do it yourself!*'

VIVIENNE WESTWOOD

Fresh is best

Unless you are feeding a football team, you really don't need a refrigerator or freezer overflowing with food. Buy smaller quantities of fresh produce and enjoy your food while it's at its best.

'No act of kindness,
however small,
is ever wasted.'

AESOP

Get in touch

Don't put off getting in touch with a friend until you have time. If you find yourself thinking of someone, call them. Don't let being busy be your excuse.

Now is the perfect time to get in touch, no matter how briefly.

*'A good laugh is sunshine
in the house.'*

WILLIAM THACKERAY

Fill it with laughter

There is little to be gained by filling your home with things: gadgets, widgets and the latest technology. No matter how exciting these can sound, all too often they won't be used enough to have been worth the investment.

If you really want to improve the quality of your life, save your money and fill your home with love and laughter instead.

*'Too many people spend money
they haven't earned,
to buy things they don't want,
to impress people they don't like.'*

WILL ROGERS

Save your money

When you find yourself tempted to buy something you can't really afford, ask yourself, *'Who am I buying this for?'*

Although the obvious answer might be *'me'*, on closer inspection you will likely find that there is someone else you were hoping to impress with your purchase.

'It is not how much we have,
but how much we enjoy,
that makes happiness.'

CHARLES SPURGEON

Don't keep it for best

If you find yourself putting things aside and saving them for good – be that homewares, clothing, jewellery or any other possessions – stop and ask yourself, 'What is stopping me from using this today?'

Rather than saving things for 'good', use the things you love all the time and make every day a special day.

'Clear your mind of can't.'

SAMUEL JOHNSON

Press delete

One of the most debilitating and destructive words in the English language is 'can't'. It gets in the way of so much potential. Delete 'can't' from your vocabulary and start thinking of all that you can.

*'True silence is the rest of the mind,
and is to the spirit what sleep is to the body,
nourishment and refreshment.'*

WILLIAM PENN

Learn to meditate

You don't need to sit cross-legged and chant '*om*' to meditate.

True meditation is simply taking the time to be silent and alone with your thoughts, then allowing those thoughts to be set free.

'*Together in our house,*
in the firelight,
we are the world made small.'

JENNIFER DONNELLY

Treasure your loved ones

It's easy to let other things get in the way
of spending time together as a family – a
stressful day at work, a big deadline, a new
romance or a busy social life.

No matter what distractions are competing
for your attention, nothing is more important
than family. Treasure yours and make them a
priority in your life.

'The key is in not spending time,
but in investing it.'

STEPHEN R. COVEY

Create a list

It's a fact of life that certain things need doing again, again and again.

Rather than reinvent the wheel every time something needs doing, spend the time to make a list. You will only have to do this once. You can then save your brainpower for something else while you work your way through checking it off.

'One's destination is never a place,
but a new way of seeing things.'

HENRY MILLER

Enhance your experience

When you go somewhere new for the first time, look around you to see what you can discover.

Of course there is often plenty to learn about art, history or culture. But just as interesting are the simple observations you can make about the way people are living their lives – observations you can then use to enhance your own life in some way on your return.

'Ability is what you're capable of doing.
Motivation determines what you do.
Attitude determines how well you do it.'

LOU HOLTZ

Have a good attitude

You don't have to do everything to get ahead in life. What you do need to do is a great job of the things you decide to do.

Even if your skills for a certain task are really quite basic, it will be your attitude and effort in doing it that will make all the difference.

'In seeking happiness for others,
you find it for yourself.'

ANONYMOUS

Don't be selfish

You don't need to be selfless to be a good friend, but you need to avoid being selfish.

There is a big difference between trying to keep everyone happy and not having any regard for other people's feelings. Be considerate in your relationships and give as much as you hope to receive.

'Organisation isn't about perfection;
it's about efficiency, reducing stress and clutter,
saving time and money, and
improving your overall quality of life.'

CHRISTINA SCALISE

Done is better than perfect

Don't get so focused on your process or organisational systems that you never get around to benefiting from them.

Remind yourself that done is better than perfect. Get started and then make little improvements as you go.

*'Worry does not empty
tomorrow of its sorrow,
it empties today of its strength.'*

CORRIE TEN BOOM

Save your energy

Although it can feel like the only option, worrying and tying yourself in knots doesn't actually change anything. It can't prevent something from happening and it can't fix something that has. All it actually does is reduce the amount of energy you have to deal with whatever it is that is causing your concern.

When you find yourself worrying, stop and put your energy to better use by either addressing the issue or moving on from it.

'If you judge people,
you have no time to love them.

MOTHER TERESA

Don't be critical

Don't waste your time criticising other people.

Instead of trying to make yourself feel better by pointing out what is wrong with someone else, focus on what both you and they are getting right.

*'Nothing great was ever achieved
without enthusiasm.'*

RALPH WALDO EMERSON

Be enthusiastic

Don't ever let a lack of money stop you getting what you want out of life. While money is always helpful, it's not the only ingredient to success. All the money in the world won't achieve much without commitment and enthusiasm.

Your most valuable resources are free. Harness them and make your dreams a reality.

'Life is like riding a bicycle.
To keep your balance,
you must keep moving.'

ALBERT EINSTEIN

Try new things

Avoid getting stuck in a rut. Although doing the same thing over and over can offer some minor comfort, to live a truly balanced life you need to fill it with a variety of experiences.

Make a point of trying new things. You don't have to like every single one of them, but it's only through experience that you'll know what you do enjoy.

'If all you can do is crawl,
start crawling.'

RUMI

Take small steps

Every achievement in life begins at the beginning, so don't be put off by the gap between where you are now and where you want to get.

Ask yourself, 'What is one small thing I can do that will take me one step closer to my goal?' If you keep this up, over time these little steps will add up to a giant leap.

'Fashions fade,
style is eternal.'

YVES SAINT LAURENT

Be stylish

Don't worry about keeping up with each season's trends. You don't need to be a slave to fashion to look good. Instead, define your personal style and work out what suits you and what doesn't.

Once you know what works for you, you will always look stylish, regardless of what fashion dictates.

*'Healing is a matter of time,
but it is sometimes also
a matter of opportunity.'*

HIPPOCRATES

Rest up

If you are feeling unwell, rest.

It's such a simple notion, but something people rarely do. If you try to soldier on through an illness, you will usually just make it last longer. But if you can stop, rest and allow your body to heal, your recovery will be complete in no time.

'The more you eat, the less flavour;
the less you eat, the more flavour.'

CHINESE PROVERB

Stop when you've had enough

Despite what you may have been told as a child, finishing everything on your plate – just because it's there – isn't such a good idea. There is nothing pleasant about feeling overly full or uncomfortable.

Learn to eat slowly, enjoy each bite and remember to stop when you've had enough.

'Your relationships with others
are always a direct reflection
of the relationship you
have with yourself.'

MICHAEL THOMAS SUNNARBORG

Love yourself

When you find yourself criticising a friend, stop. Most of the time, the things we find most annoying about others are mirrors of the qualities we like least about ourselves.

Before you judge a friend for not being perfect, take a moment to forgive yourself the same.

'It's not enough to be busy,
so are the ants.
The question is, what are we busy about?'

HENRY DAVID THOREAU

Stick to the schedule

Staying on top of all the things you need to do around the home can feel overwhelming. Rather than spending your time doing the same thing over and over or – worse – living in a mess, create a routine for all your regular domestic tasks and stick to it.

You will enjoy being in your home so much more when you know that everything is taken care of.

'*A man who both spends
and saves money
is the happiest man,
because he has both enjoyments.*'

SAMUEL JOHNSON

Learn to save

Don't spend money you don't have. Most people spend too much of their income paying off things that they couldn't actually afford and didn't really need.

If you can't afford to pay for something, instead of putting it on your credit card, add it to your want list and save for it. More often than not, by the time you get your money together, you'll realise you didn't need it anyway. And if you find you do still want it, you'll then be able to comfortably afford it.

'Happiness resides not in possessions,
and not in gold,
happiness dwells in the soul.'

DEMOCRITUS

Find happiness within

Whenever you find yourself thinking, 'I'd be happy if only I had …', stop and ask yourself, 'What is stopping me from being happy today?'

True happiness can't be bought. It has to be found within. Find yours.

'Continuous effort
— not strength or intelligence —
is the key to unlocking our potential.'

Winston Churchill

Unlock your potential

Don't ever tell yourself that you're not good enough.

Whether or not you're good is all but irrelevant. All that matters is that you take the raw material you've got and then keep working at it until you get to where you want to go.

'I would rather my heart
be without words
than my words
be without heart.'

LaMar Boschman

Be a quiet comfort

We are all faced with situations in life where it's hard to know what the right thing is to say to someone. But if you don't know what to say, say so.

Being honest about your loss for words is so much more comforting than opening your mouth and letting any words that come to you spill out just to fill the space.

*'[Kids] don't remember
what you try to teach them.
They remember what you are.'*

JIM HENSON

Set an example

You can lecture a child all you like, but your words will never have the same impact as your actions.

If you want to teach a child, you have to lead by example and model the behaviour you want them to learn.

'He who does not get fun and
enjoyment out of every day ...
needs to reorganise his life.'

GEORGE M. ADAMS

Do what you want

It's easy to fill your time with all the things you think you *should* be doing, but unless you make the time for the things you *want* to be doing, all you're really doing is wasting time.

Of course there are things in life that you *have* to do, but as soon as they're done, spend your time doing what you want.

'A man travels the world over in search of what he needs and returns home to find it.'

GEORGE AUGUSTUS MOORE

Pack light

When you travel, instead of stuffing your suitcase so full you have to sit on it to close it, challenge yourself to pack light.

Lay everything out before you pack it, making sure you are taking what you need and no more. Make sure the things you include work well together, allowing you to create a travel wardrobe where the whole is greater than the sum of its parts.

*'If you look for perfection,
you'll never be content.'*

LEO TOLSTOY

Do your best

There really is no such thing as perfection.
It's entirely subjective, which makes it an
impossible goal. Remind yourself that as long
as you do your best, your best will always be
good enough.

DOMONIQUE BERTOLUCCI

*'You wouldn't worry so much
about what others think of you
if you realised how seldom they do.'*

ELEANOR ROOSEVELT

Be confident

If you are feeling nervous or self-conscious about a social situation, there really is no reason to.

If you find yourself worrying what other people think, stop. They're far too busy worrying what you think about them to be bothered thinking about you.

*'There is nothing quite so useless
as doing with great efficiency
something that should not be done at all.'*

PETER F. DRUCKER

Cross it off

Before you get started on your to-do list,
have a look and see what you can cross off it.

Get rid of all the things you think you
should do and all the things that you *could* do
and then focus on the much shorter list of
things that simply have to be done.

*'If things start happening,
don't worry, don't stew,
just go right along and
you'll start happening too.'*

DR. SEUSS

Go with the flow

One of the biggest causes of stress is trying to force things to turn out the way you want them to. The truth is that in life, some things will go your way and unfortunately others won't.

Rather than trying to force the outcome you want, look at how you can work with things the way they actually are.

'The real lover is the man who can
thrill you by kissing your forehead or
smiling into your eyes or
just staring into space.'

MARILYN MONROE

Be loving and kind

There is more to lasting love than passion and romance. Grand gestures are all well and good, but it's the little things that matter: thoughtful words, a helping hand, a sign of acknowledgement or appreciation, an affectionate embrace and companionable silence.

Passion fades and romance won't always be there, but kind and loving gestures will help to keep your love alive over time.

'Doing good can be as simple as
leaving one human being
in better shape than you found them.'

ALEXANDRA FRANZEN

Make a difference

If you want to make the world a better place, do it.

There's no need to wait until you have achieved this or have done that. The way to make a difference is through one good deed at a time. Start with the little things and start today.

Acknowledgements

M Y FIRST THANKS, as always, go to my wonderful agent, Tara Wynne at Curtis Brown, for her never-ending belief in my work. Thank you to Fran Berry and the team at Hardie Grant for once again being such a delight to work with.

To all my clients, past and present, the inspiring people who attend my workshops and those who buy my online programs, thank you. I love my work and it is in no small part because I get to share it with you.

To my readers who connect with me on my Facebook page, thank you for sharing your experiences or simply stopping by to say hello. It means the world to me.

Less is more in so many things but not when it comes to support, and I wouldn't be able to do all that I do if I didn't have the help of Dani Magestro in my business and Nesli Acar in my home. It is wonderful to know that both my business and my children are in safe and caring hands. Thanks to Brooke Alexander for sharing so much of this journey with me.

A never-ending thank you to my mum for once again proof-reading patiently and loving unconditionally.

To my darling Sophia, precious Toby and to Paul, for everything, always.

About the Author

Domonique Bertolucci is the bestselling author of *The Happiness Code: Ten keys to being the best you can be* and six other books about happiness: what it is, how to get it and, most importantly, how to keep it.

Domonique has spent the last twenty-five years working with large companies, dynamic small businesses and everyday people, teaching them how to get more happiness, more success and more time just to catch their breath.

Prior to starting her own business in 2003, Domonique worked in the cut-throat world of high finance, where she gained a reputation as a strategic problem solver and dynamic leader. In her final corporate role, she was the most senior woman in a billion-dollar company.

Domonique's readership spans the English-speaking world, and her workshops, online courses and coach training programs are attended by people from all walks of life from all around the globe – people who want more out of life at home, at work and everywhere in between.

As well as being an accomplished professional speaker, Domonique has given hundreds of interviews across all forms of media including television, radio, print and digital media; more than 10 million people have seen, read or heard her advice.

When she is not working, Domonique's favourite ways of spending her time are with her husband and two children, reading a good book and keeping up the great Italian tradition of feeding the people that you love.

Domonique jokes that she has nearly as many passports as James Bond. She is Australian by birth, Italian by blood and British by choice. She is currently based in Sydney, Australia.

Other books by Domonique

The Happiness Code: Ten keys to being the best you can be

Love Your Life: 100 ways to start living the life you deserve

100 Days Happier: Daily inspiration for life-long happiness

Less is More: 101 ways to simplify your life

The Kindness Pact: 8 promises to make you feel good about who you are and the life you live

The Daily Promise: 100 ways to feel happy about your life

Guided journals by Domonique

Live more each day: A journal to discover what really matters

Be happy each day: A journal for life-long happiness

Keep in touch with Domonique at:

domoniquebertolucci.com
facebook.com/domoniquebertolucci
instagram.com/domoniquebertolucci

Join Domonique's private Facebook Group for regular discussion, insights and inspiration to help you get more out of life:
Facebook.com/groups/domoniquebertolucci

For more information:

Find out more about Domonique's life coaching courses and programs:
domoniquebertolucci.com/programs

Find out more about Domonique's coach training program and become a certified professional coach:
domoniquebertolucci.com/coach-training

Published in 2021 by Hardie Grant Books,
an imprint of Hardie Grant Publishing
First published in 2014

Hardie Grant Books (Melbourne)
Building 1, 658 Church Street
Richmond, Victoria 3121

Hardie Grant Books (London)
5th & 6th Floors
52–54 Southwark Street
London SE1 1UN

hardiegrantbooks.com

A catalogue record for this
book is available from the
National Library of Australia

NATIONAL LIBRARY OF AUSTRALIA

Less Is More
ISBN 978 1 74379 766 2

10 9 8 7 6 5 4 3 2 1

Cover design by Emily O'Neill
Typeset in Plantin Light 11/17 pt by Cannon Typesetting
Printed in China by Leo Paper Products LTD.

The paper this book is printed on is from
FSC®-certified forests and other sources.
FSC® promotes environmentally responsible,
socially beneficial and economically viable
management of the world's forests.

Hardie Grant acknowledges the Traditional Owners of the country on which
we work, the Wurundjeri people of the Kulin nation and the Gadigal people of
the Eora nation, and recognises their continuing connection to the land, waters
and culture. We pay our respects to their Elders past, present and emerging.